U·N·D·E·R·S·E·A

Created and written by Moira Butterfield
Designed and illustrated by Paul Johnson

Contents

Ideals Children's Books
Nashville, Tennessee

OCEANS OF THE WORLD

Salty water covers about 70 percent of the earth's surface, ranging from tropical seas as warm as bathwater to freezing water thick with icebergs. On maps the water is divided into five large areas — the Atlantic, Pacific, Indian, Antarctic, and Arctic Oceans.

The oceans are the world's biggest animal home. Many trillions of creatures live beneath the waves — from tiny amebas, too small to see, to huge blue whales. In this book, you can find out about ocean life and make your own undersea model.

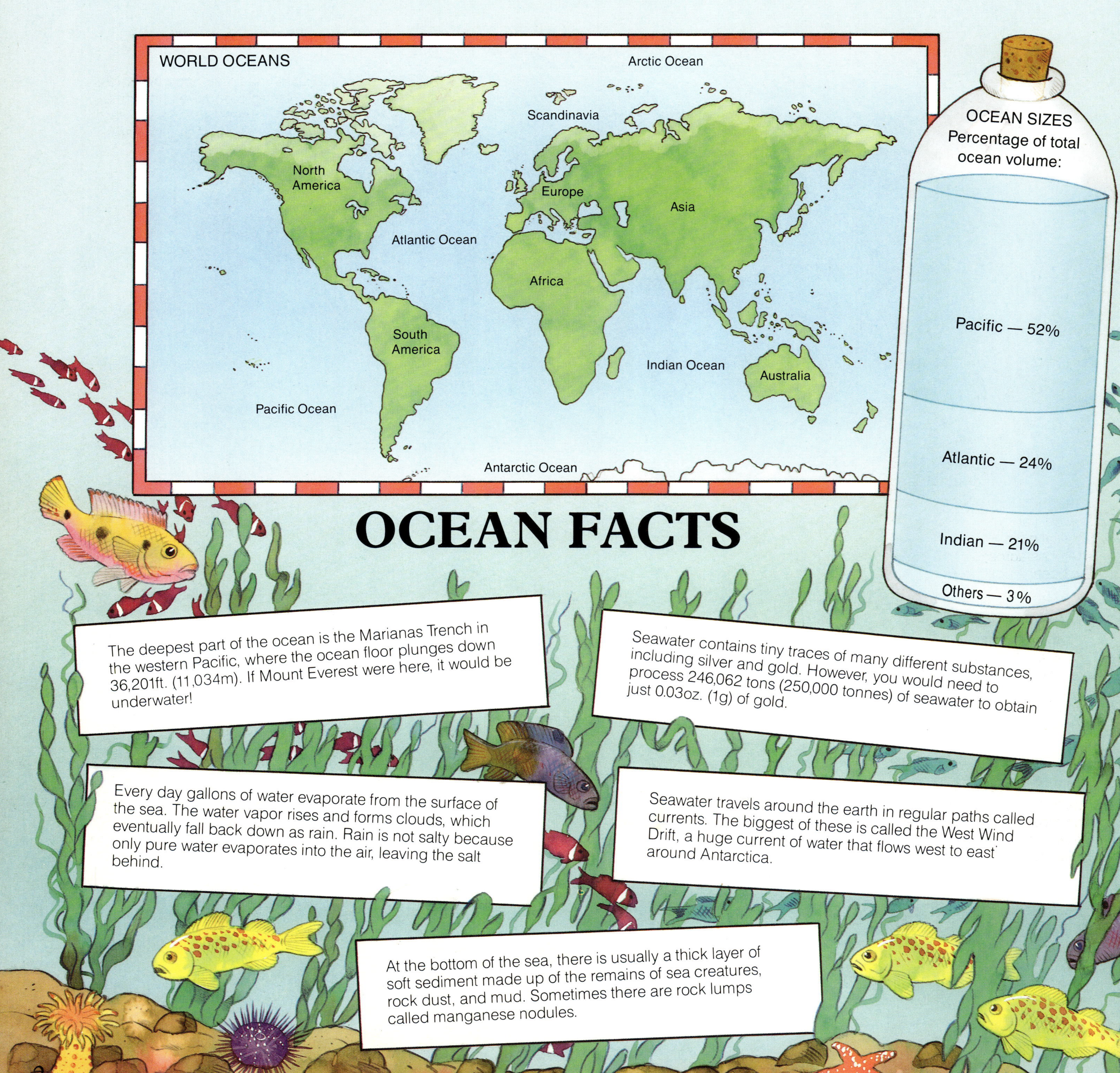

OCEAN FACTS

The deepest part of the ocean is the Marianas Trench in the western Pacific, where the ocean floor plunges down 36,201ft. (11,034m). If Mount Everest were here, it would be underwater!

Seawater contains tiny traces of many different substances, including silver and gold. However, you would need to process 246,062 tons (250,000 tonnes) of seawater to obtain just 0.03oz. (1g) of gold.

Every day gallons of water evaporate from the surface of the sea. The water vapor rises and forms clouds, which eventually fall back down as rain. Rain is not salty because only pure water evaporates into the air, leaving the salt behind.

Seawater travels around the earth in regular paths called currents. The biggest of these is called the West Wind Drift, a huge current of water that flows west to east around Antarctica.

At the bottom of the sea, there is usually a thick layer of soft sediment made up of the remains of sea creatures, rock dust, and mud. Sometimes there are rock lumps called manganese nodules.

UNDER THE SEA

Underneath the surface of the sea, there are mountains, valleys, plains, and canyons. The picture on this page shows a slice of seabed from a typical ocean.

① Around the edges of land, there is a shallow platform called the continental shelf. Sometimes valleys and canyons cut into the shelf.

The underwater Monterey Canyon cuts through the continental shelf off the coast of California. It is as deep and long as the Grand Canyon.

② The continental shelf usually slopes down to the ocean floor. This slope is called the continental rise. The Atlantic and Indian Oceans have very wide rises; but in the Pacific Ocean, rises are very narrow or nonexistent.

③ Around the edges of some oceans, there are very deep canyons called oceanic trenches, where the deepest parts of the sea are found.

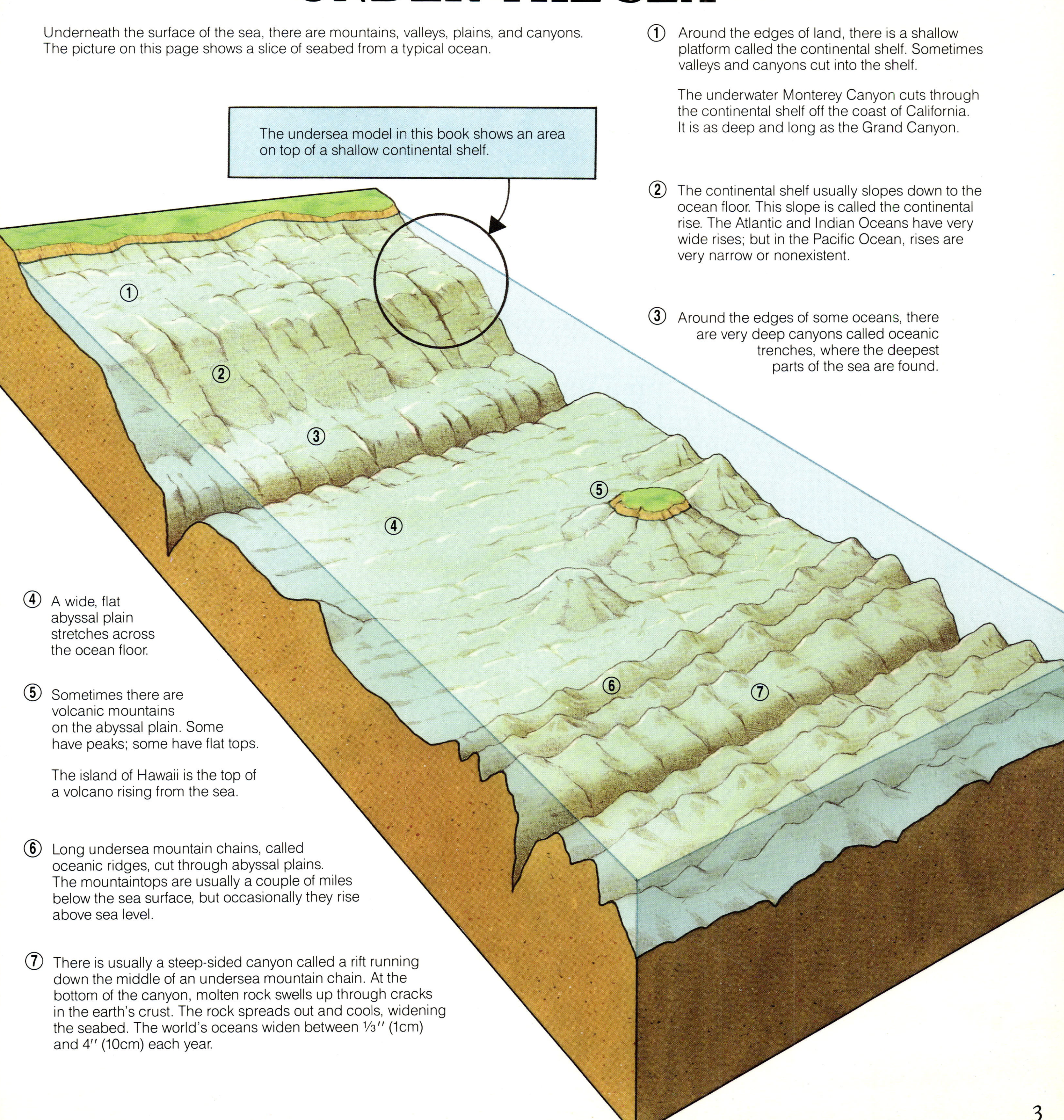

④ A wide, flat abyssal plain stretches across the ocean floor.

⑤ Sometimes there are volcanic mountains on the abyssal plain. Some have peaks; some have flat tops.

The island of Hawaii is the top of a volcano rising from the sea.

⑥ Long undersea mountain chains, called oceanic ridges, cut through abyssal plains. The mountaintops are usually a couple of miles below the sea surface, but occasionally they rise above sea level.

⑦ There is usually a steep-sided canyon called a rift running down the middle of an undersea mountain chain. At the bottom of the canyon, molten rock swells up through cracks in the earth's crust. The rock spreads out and cools, widening the seabed. The world's oceans widen between 1/3″ (1cm) and 4″ (10cm) each year.

LIFE IN THE OCEANS

There are about 160,000 different kinds, or species, of ocean animals. Some of these species have many millions of members. For instance, there are thought to be a trillion herring in the Atlantic Ocean alone!

Ocean life varies in different sea environments. Some animals live only in warm water, while others prefer cold seas. The model in this book shows creatures found mainly in warm oceans.

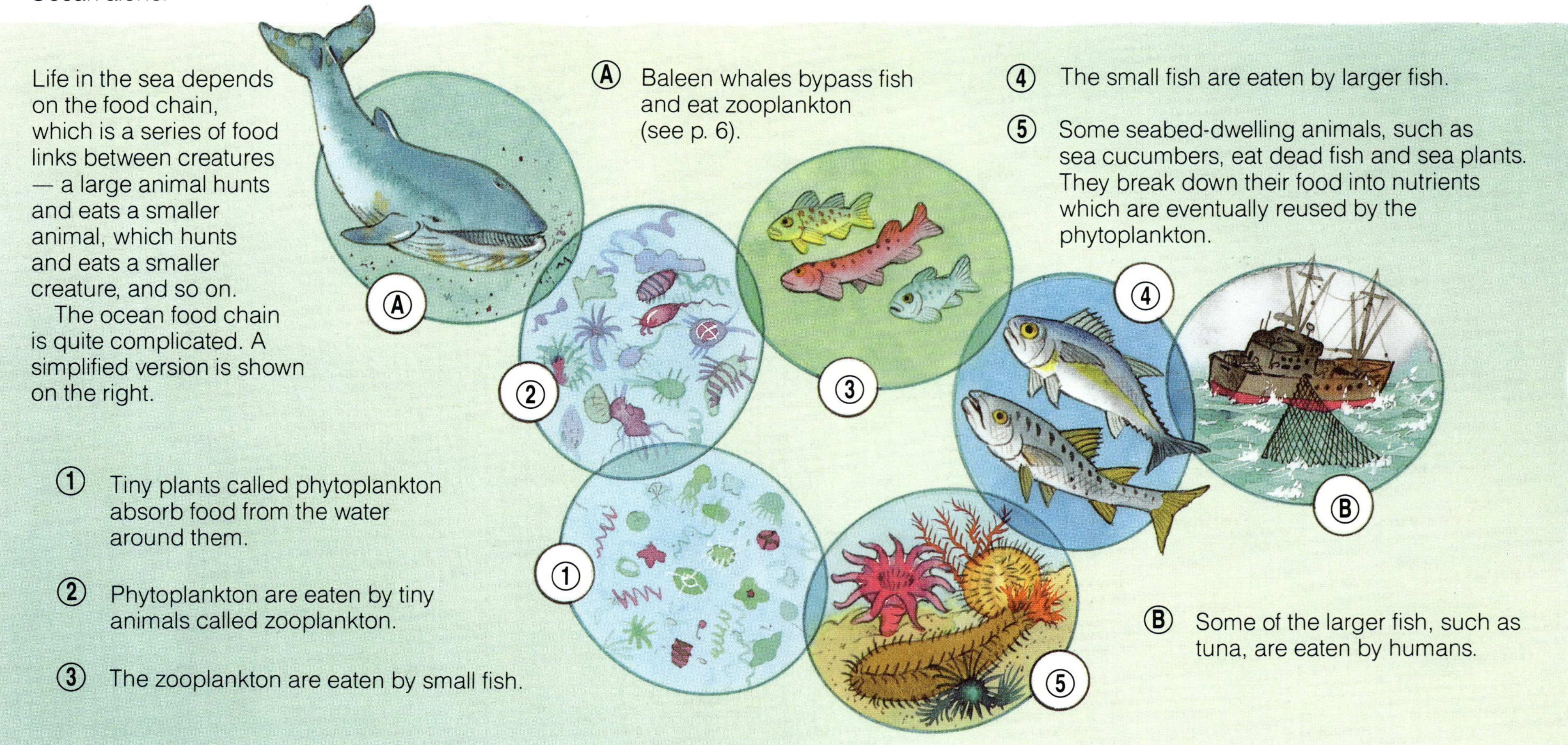

Life in the sea depends on the food chain, which is a series of food links between creatures — a large animal hunts and eats a smaller animal, which hunts and eats a smaller creature, and so on.

The ocean food chain is quite complicated. A simplified version is shown on the right.

① Tiny plants called phytoplankton absorb food from the water around them.

② Phytoplankton are eaten by tiny animals called zooplankton.

③ The zooplankton are eaten by small fish.

Ⓐ Baleen whales bypass fish and eat zooplankton (see p. 6).

④ The small fish are eaten by larger fish.

⑤ Some seabed-dwelling animals, such as sea cucumbers, eat dead fish and sea plants. They break down their food into nutrients which are eventually reused by the phytoplankton.

Ⓑ Some of the larger fish, such as tuna, are eaten by humans.

OCEAN HOMES

Many sea animals spend their lives near the water surface. These areas are often called the ''pastures of the sea,'' because food is so plentiful there.

Rocks provide an anchor for animals such as barnacles and anemones. They make good hiding places for secretive creatures such as moray eels.

Sunlight shines down into the sea, but the deeper the water, the darker it gets. Deeper than about 3280ft. (1000m), the water is inky black. Creatures who live in the darkness often produce their own light (see p. 7).

Coral reefs are found in shallow, warm seas. They are made up of many tiny creatures called polyps, all joined together. Some polyps have a hard coating; some are soft. Reefs are usually teeming with wildlife.

Shipwrecks are colonized by all kinds of sea animals.

On the flat seabed, creatures burrow beneath the muddy ooze or crawl along, feeding on decaying matter. Sea cucumbers, worms, and crabs may be found here.

FISH

There are about 20,000 species of ocean fish. Most have streamlined bodies, so that they can slip easily through the water, and fins and a tail to help them steer as they swim.

Most fish belong to the "bony" group, which means that they have an internal skeleton of bones. The coral trout in the model is an example.

Bony fish usually have an air-filled sac called a swim bladder inside their bodies. This helps to keep them afloat.

Sharks, rays, and skates belong to the "cartilaginous" group of fish. Instead of bones, they have body frames made of thick, gristly muscle. They don't have swim bladders, so they must keep moving all the time or else they will sink!

Coral trout

Whale shark

Coral reef fish

The world's biggest fish, the whale shark, can grow up to 49 ft (15m) long. It is found in warm parts of the Pacific, Atlantic, and Indian Oceans. By contrast, the world's smallest fish is the dwarf goby, found in the Indian Ocean. It is no bigger than the size of a human thumbnail.

Some fish are very colorful, especially those species that live around coral reefs. Often the color is for camouflage — the fish seem to merge with the background, making them difficult for enemies to see. There are also fish that can change color to blend with different backgrounds.

CRUSTACEANS

Crabs, lobsters, shrimp, and barnacles all belong to a group of animals called crustaceans. This group ranges from microscopic floating creatures to giant lobsters weighing 28½ pounds (13kg) and crabs with legs measuring 5ft. (1.5m) long.

Most crustaceans have a hard coat of some kind. For instance, crabs have a brittle shell, and barnacles live inside a rock-hard cloak of limestone.

Crustaceans

ECHINODERMS

Starfish are not really fish at all! Together with sea urchins, brittle stars, and sea cucumbers, they make up an ocean animal group called echinoderms, which means "spiny-skinned." Echinoderms do not have brains. Instead they have a network of nerves running around the body.

Starfish attack and eat shellfish. The starfish fastens onto a shell and uses strong tube feet to pull it open.

Echinoderms

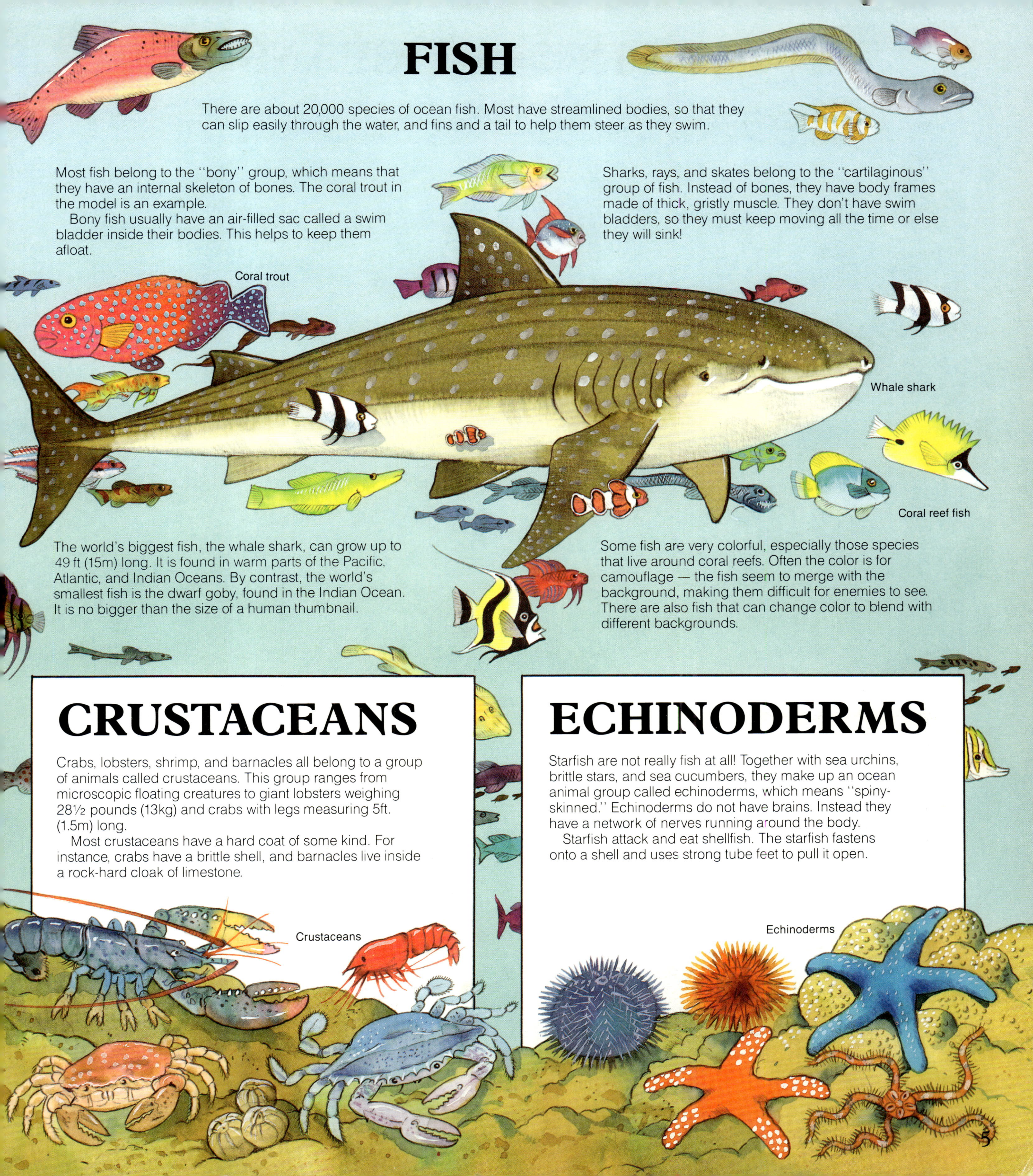

SEA MAMMALS

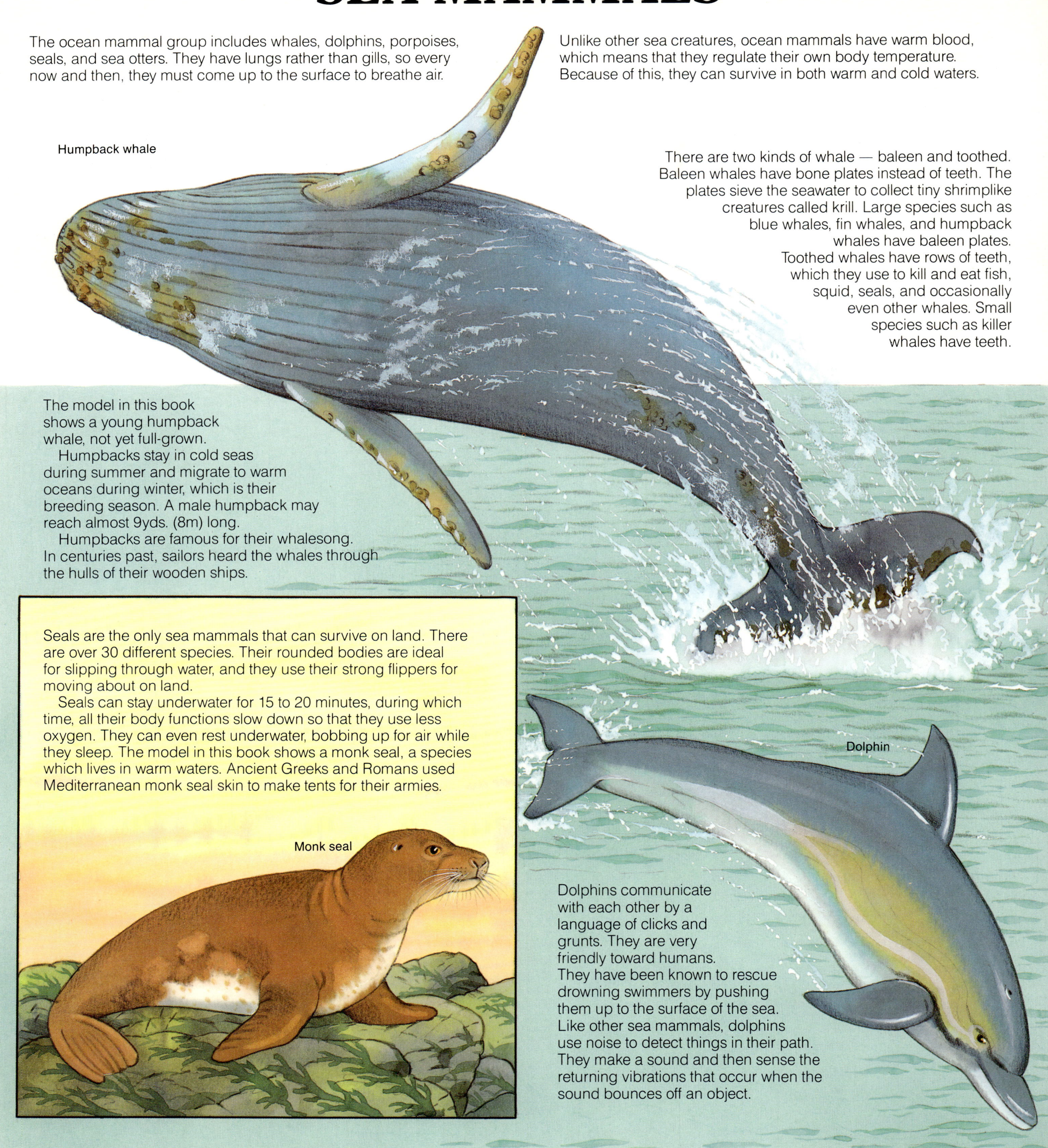

The ocean mammal group includes whales, dolphins, porpoises, seals, and sea otters. They have lungs rather than gills, so every now and then, they must come up to the surface to breathe air.

Unlike other sea creatures, ocean mammals have warm blood, which means that they regulate their own body temperature. Because of this, they can survive in both warm and cold waters.

There are two kinds of whale — baleen and toothed. Baleen whales have bone plates instead of teeth. The plates sieve the seawater to collect tiny shrimplike creatures called krill. Large species such as blue whales, fin whales, and humpback whales have baleen plates. Toothed whales have rows of teeth, which they use to kill and eat fish, squid, seals, and occasionally even other whales. Small species such as killer whales have teeth.

The model in this book shows a young humpback whale, not yet full-grown.

Humpbacks stay in cold seas during summer and migrate to warm oceans during winter, which is their breeding season. A male humpback may reach almost 9yds. (8m) long.

Humpbacks are famous for their whalesong. In centuries past, sailors heard the whales through the hulls of their wooden ships.

Seals are the only sea mammals that can survive on land. There are over 30 different species. Their rounded bodies are ideal for slipping through water, and they use their strong flippers for moving about on land.

Seals can stay underwater for 15 to 20 minutes, during which time, all their body functions slow down so that they use less oxygen. They can even rest underwater, bobbing up for air while they sleep. The model in this book shows a monk seal, a species which lives in warm waters. Ancient Greeks and Romans used Mediterranean monk seal skin to make tents for their armies.

Dolphins communicate with each other by a language of clicks and grunts. They are very friendly toward humans. They have been known to rescue drowning swimmers by pushing them up to the surface of the sea. Like other sea mammals, dolphins use noise to detect things in their path. They make a sound and then sense the returning vibrations that occur when the sound bounces off an object.

DANGEROUS CREATURES

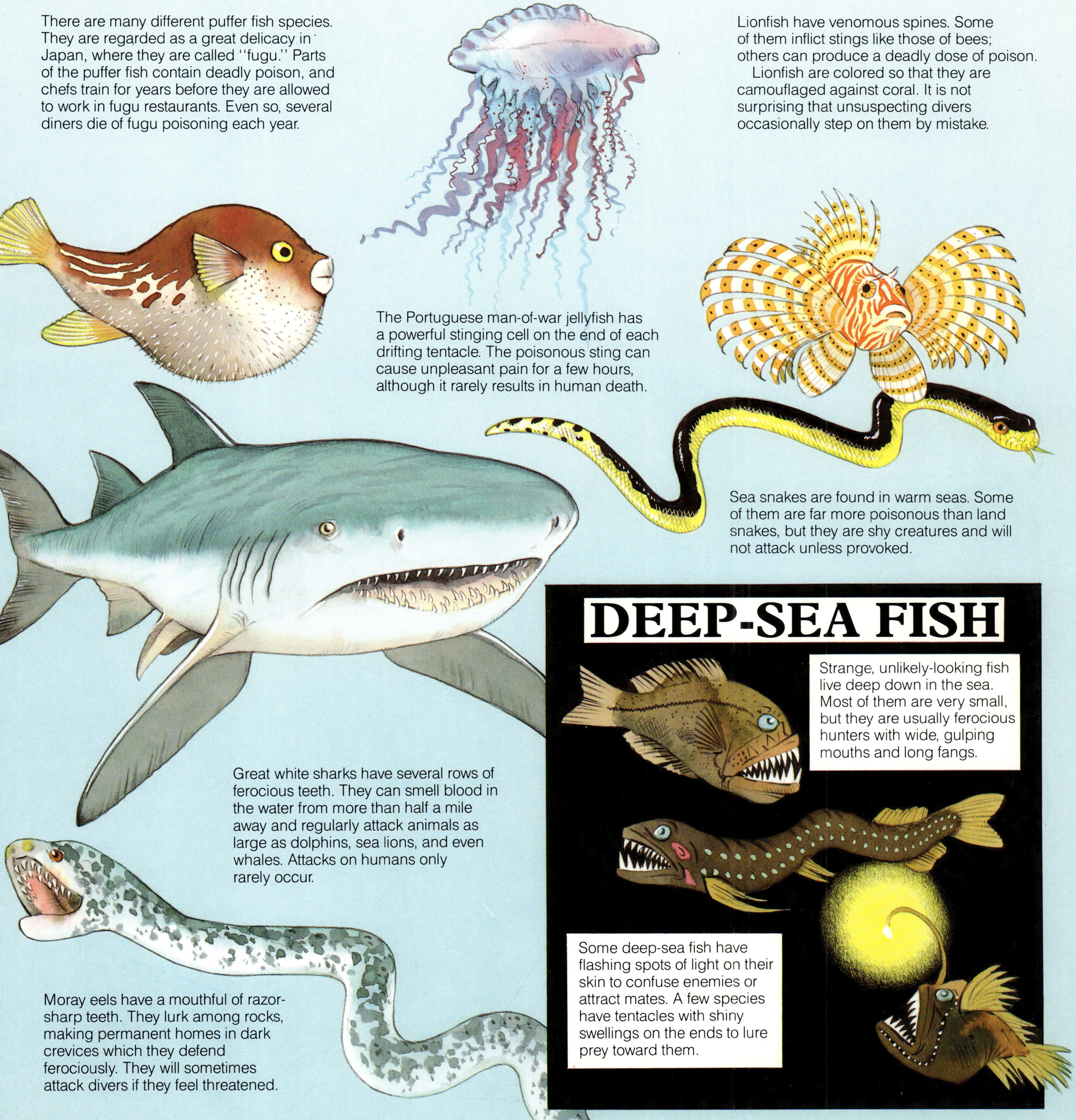

There are many different puffer fish species. They are regarded as a great delicacy in Japan, where they are called "fugu." Parts of the puffer fish contain deadly poison, and chefs train for years before they are allowed to work in fugu restaurants. Even so, several diners die of fugu poisoning each year.

The Portuguese man-of-war jellyfish has a powerful stinging cell on the end of each drifting tentacle. The poisonous sting can cause unpleasant pain for a few hours, although it rarely results in human death.

Lionfish have venomous spines. Some of them inflict stings like those of bees; others can produce a deadly dose of poison. Lionfish are colored so that they are camouflaged against coral. It is not surprising that unsuspecting divers occasionally step on them by mistake.

Sea snakes are found in warm seas. Some of them are far more poisonous than land snakes, but they are shy creatures and will not attack unless provoked.

Great white sharks have several rows of ferocious teeth. They can smell blood in the water from more than half a mile away and regularly attack animals as large as dolphins, sea lions, and even whales. Attacks on humans only rarely occur.

Moray eels have a mouthful of razor-sharp teeth. They lurk among rocks, making permanent homes in dark crevices which they defend ferociously. They will sometimes attack divers if they feel threatened.

DEEP-SEA FISH

Strange, unlikely-looking fish live deep down in the sea. Most of them are very small, but they are usually ferocious hunters with wide, gulping mouths and long fangs.

Some deep-sea fish have flashing spots of light on their skin to confuse enemies or attract mates. A few species have tentacles with shiny swellings on the ends to lure prey toward them.

AMAZING ANIMALS

Here are some facts about the more unusual sea animals in the press-out model.

Arctic terns make one of the longest journeys in the animal kingdom. In the summer, they breed in the Arctic. When September comes, they set off on a round-the-world trip to Antarctica, returning to the Arctic the following June.

Arctic tern

Wandering albatross

There are several albatross species. The wandering albatross is the largest, with a wingspan measuring up to 10ft. (3.15m approx.). Albatrosses rarely alight on land. When night falls, they bob up and down on the sea surface. They depend on the wind to help them take off, so on calm days they find it quite difficult to fly.

Turtles have flippers instead of legs. They can swim very fast in the water. Female green turtles swim to land to lay their eggs in holes on sandy beaches. When the tiny turtles hatch, they crawl as quickly as they can toward the sea.

Green turtle

There are about 400 species of squid. The giant squid may grow tentacles as long as 49ft. (15m)! Squid have their own propulsion system. They take in water and squirt it out at high pressure through nozzles on their bodies.

Giant squid

There are about 150 octopus species. They can all camouflage themselves, changing the colors and patterns on their skin to blend in with almost any background.

Octopus

Flying fish live in warm seas, where they feed on plankton. They glide above the sea surface when they want to avoid predators, swimming upward quickly and taking off with a flick of the tail. They can glide for up to half a minute.

Flying fish

PEOPLE AND THE SEA

Divers can explore shallow seas by using scuba gear, which allows them to breathe underwater. Wearing scuba tanks filled with compressed air, divers breathe in air as they need it.

Underwater vehicles called submersibles are ideal for exploring the ocean floor. Manned submersibles have an oxygen-supply inside. They have lights and robot arms outside.

Diving archaeologists study shipwrecks. They must do their work very carefully; the objects they find are often valuable clues to life in the past.

CONSERVING THE SEAS

The world's oceans are threatened by pollution and overfishing. Here are some examples of efforts being made to halt the damage.

Some animal species have become endangered because of overfishing or pollution. The large whales are the most threatened group, along with turtles, seals, dolphins, and a variety of seabirds. Many countries have signed agreements limiting fishing and whale hunting.

Many seas have been polluted by oil, factory waste, and sewage. Some international laws have been passed to try to limit the damage.

Divers can damage coral reefs by taking coral or killing wildlife. To prevent this, some reefs have been made nature reserves where diving is carefully controlled. You can help stop the damage by refusing to buy pieces of coral or rare shells which have been taken from reefs.

HOW TO MAKE YOUR MODEL

Start by carefully opening the staples in the middle of the book. Lift out the two middle sheets, A and B, which have model pieces on them. Then close the staples to make the book complete again. Press out each model piece as you need it.

① Press out the base ①. It has some slits stamped on it. Press them open and lay the base flat on a tabletop.

Sheet A

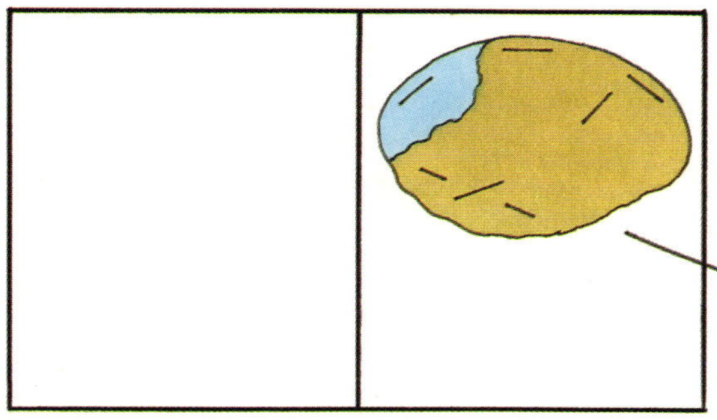

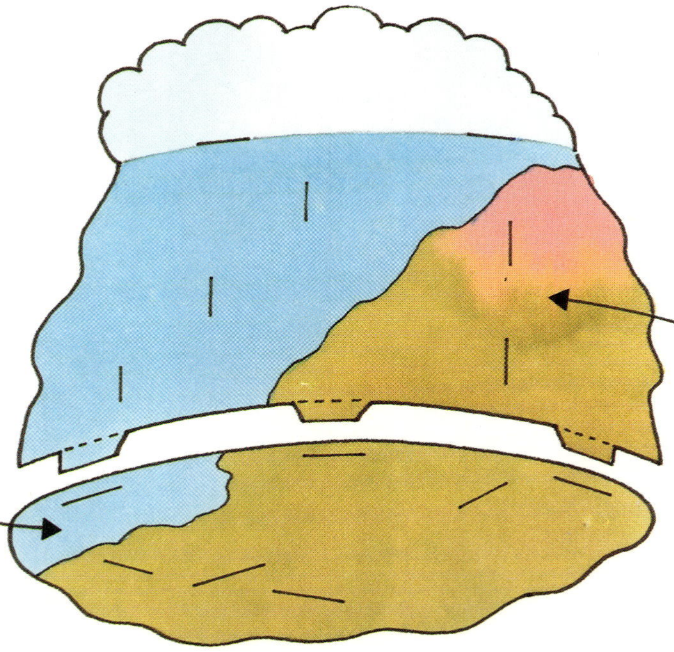

② Press out the background ② and make sure that the slits on it are pressed open. Push the flaps on the bottom of the backdrop into the slits at the back of the base. Then bend the flaps so that they lie flat. You can glue or tape them if you want to make your model permanent.

Sheet A

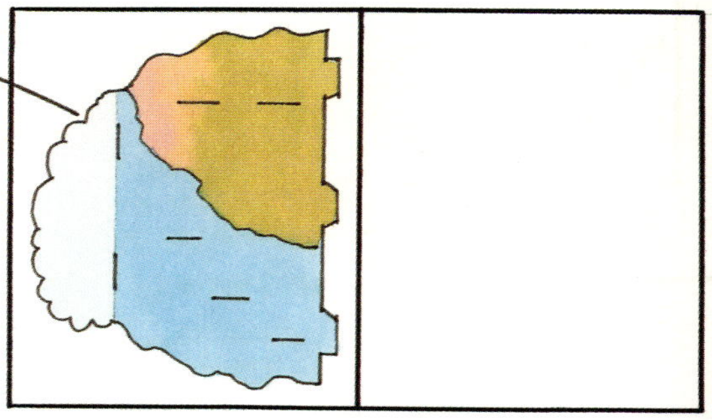

③ Press out the foreground ③ and make sure that the slits on it are pressed open. Push the bottom flaps into the slits on the base and fold them so that they lie flat. Push the flaps on the right-hand side into the slits on the background.

Sheet B

Sheet B

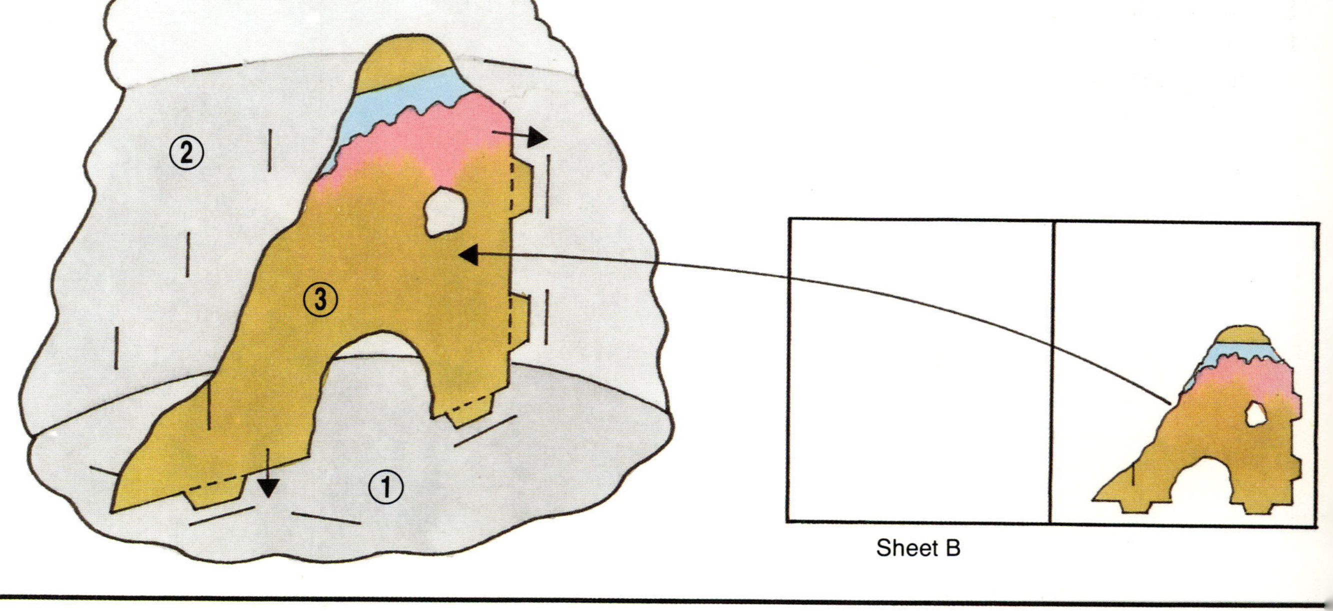

④ Before you add any larger pieces, you need to add some small details. Press out the coral trout, the angel fish and the deep-sea fish. Push them into the three slits on the left-hand side of the background.

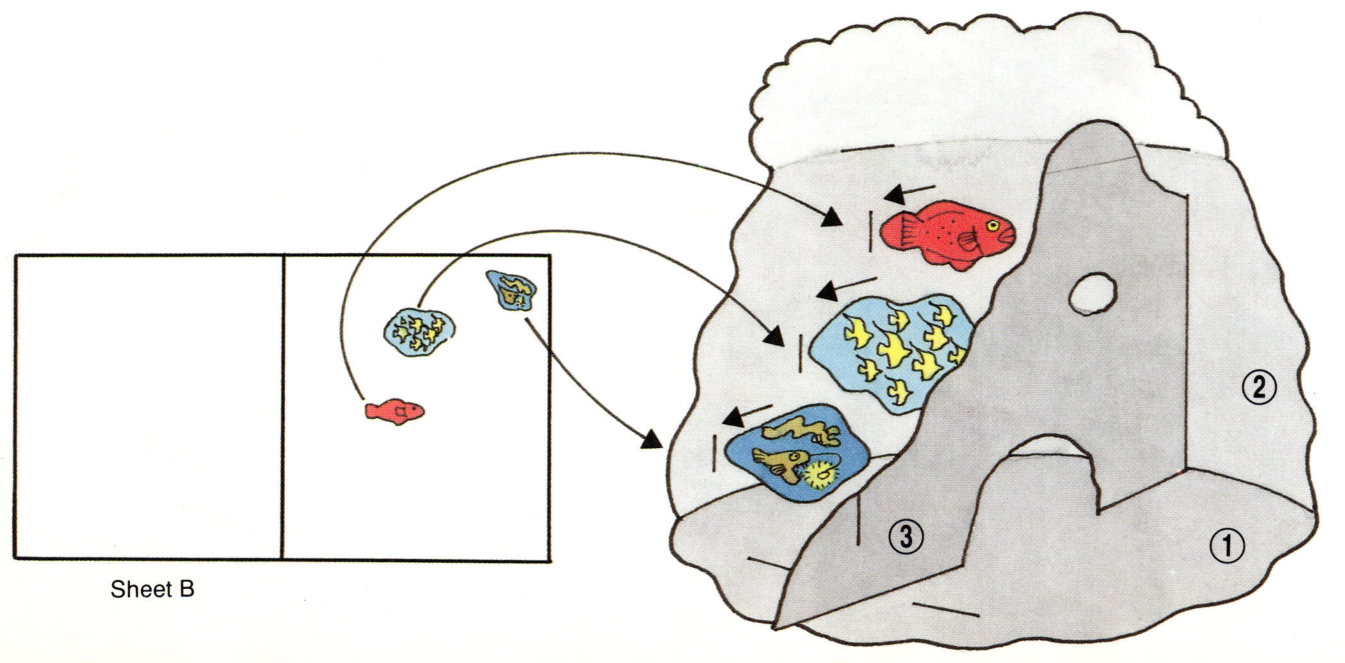

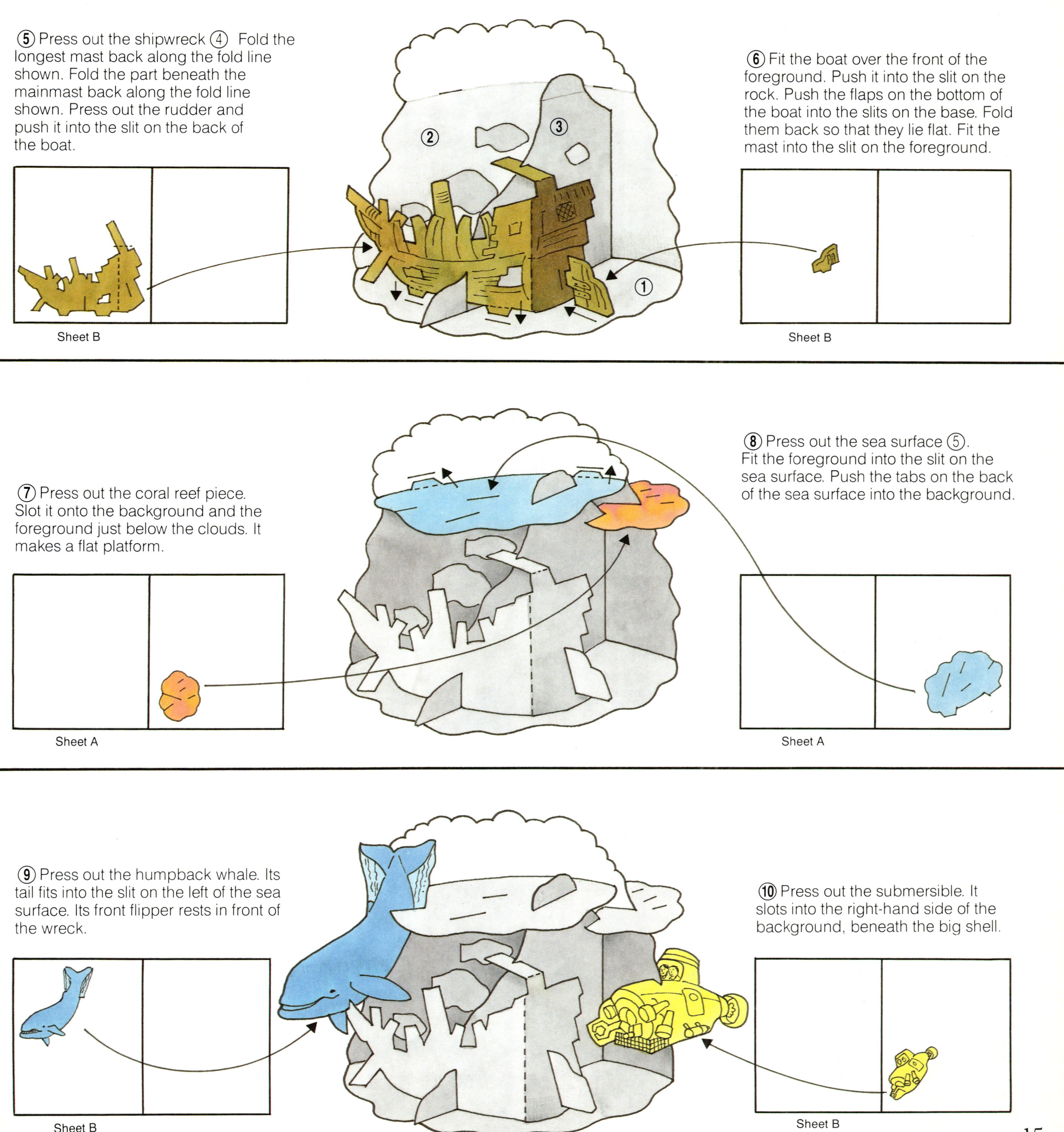

⑤ Press out the shipwreck ④ Fold the longest mast back along the fold line shown. Fold the part beneath the mainmast back along the fold line shown. Press out the rudder and push it into the slit on the back of the boat.

⑥ Fit the boat over the front of the foreground. Push it into the slit on the rock. Push the flaps on the bottom of the boat into the slits on the base. Fold them back so that they lie flat. Fit the mast into the slit on the foreground.

⑦ Press out the coral reef piece. Slot it onto the background and the foreground just below the clouds. It makes a flat platform.

⑧ Press out the sea surface ⑤. Fit the foreground into the slit on the sea surface. Push the tabs on the back of the sea surface into the background.

⑨ Press out the humpback whale. Its tail fits into the slit on the left of the sea surface. Its front flipper rests in front of the wreck.

⑩ Press out the submersible. It slots into the right-hand side of the background, beneath the big shell.

15

SEALIFE

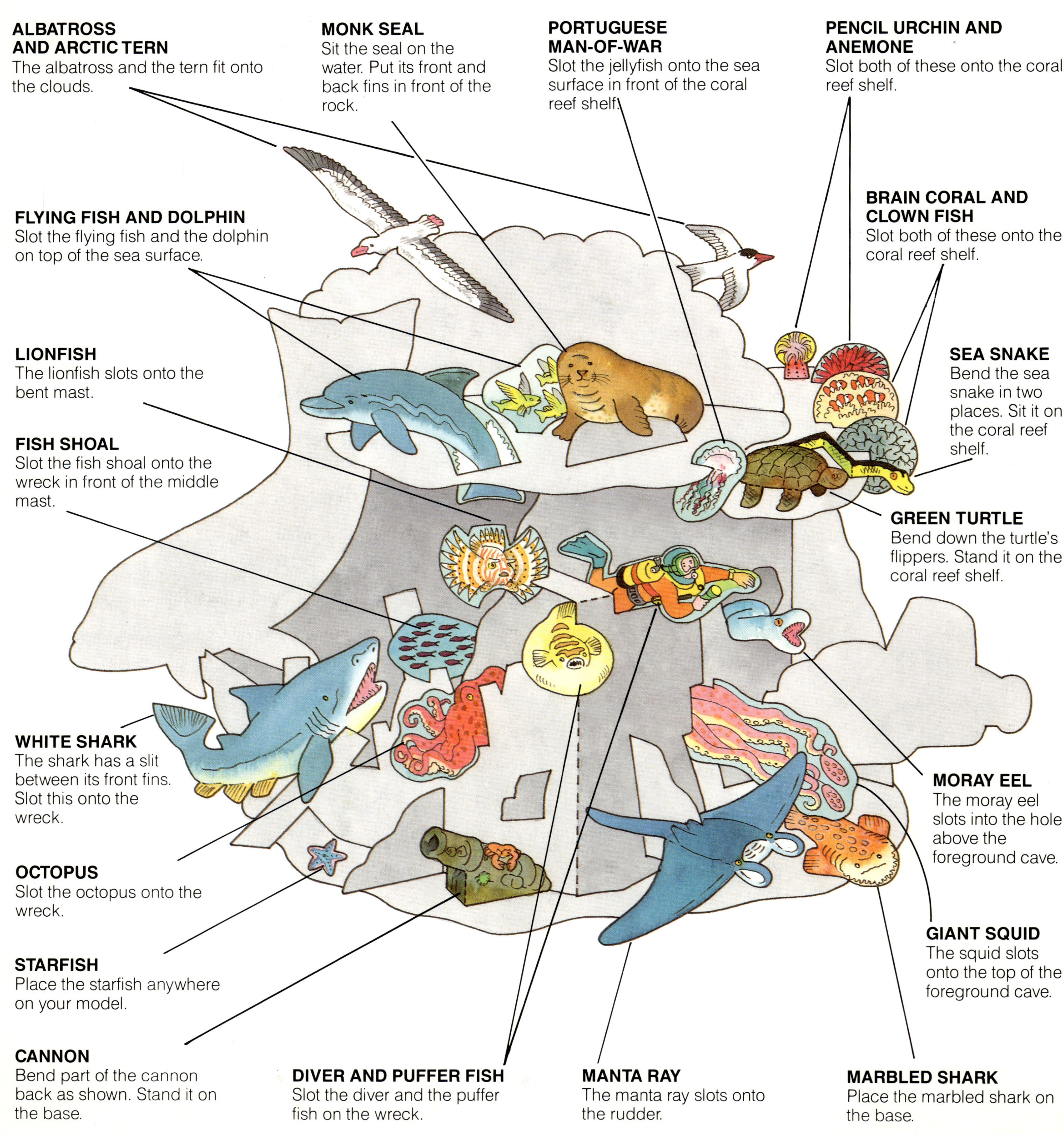

ALBATROSS
AND ARCTIC TERN
The albatross and the tern fit onto
the clouds.

MONK SEAL
Sit the seal on the
water. Put its front and
back fins in front of the
rock.

PORTUGUESE
MAN-OF-WAR
Slot the jellyfish onto the sea
surface in front of the coral
reef shelf.

PENCIL URCHIN AND
ANEMONE
Slot both of these onto the coral
reef shelf.

FLYING FISH AND DOLPHIN
Slot the flying fish and the dolphin
on top of the sea surface.

BRAIN CORAL AND
CLOWN FISH
Slot both of these onto the
coral reef shelf.

LIONFISH
The lionfish slots onto the
bent mast.

SEA SNAKE
Bend the sea
snake in two
places. Sit it on
the coral reef
shelf.

FISH SHOAL
Slot the fish shoal onto the
wreck in front of the middle
mast.

GREEN TURTLE
Bend down the turtle's
flippers. Stand it on the
coral reef shelf.

WHITE SHARK
The shark has a slit
between its front fins.
Slot this onto the
wreck.

MORAY EEL
The moray eel
slots into the hole
above the
foreground cave.

OCTOPUS
Slot the octopus onto the
wreck.

STARFISH
Place the starfish anywhere
on your model.

GIANT SQUID
The squid slots
onto the top of the
foreground cave.

CANNON
Bend part of the cannon
back as shown. Stand it on
the base.

DIVER AND PUFFER FISH
Slot the diver and the puffer
fish on the wreck.

MANTA RAY
The manta ray slots onto
the rudder.

MARBLED SHARK
Place the marbled shark on
the base.

16